VICKIE GILL

The
TEN COMMANDMENTS
of
PROFESSIONALISM
for TEACHERS

WISDOM FROM A VETERAN TEACHER

CORWIN PRESS
A Sage Publications Company
Thousand Oaks, California

For information:

Corwin Press
A Sage Publications Company
2455 Teller Road
Thousand Oaks, California 91320
www.corwinpress.com

Sage Publications Ltd.
1 Oliver's Yard
55 City Road
London EC1Y 1SP
United Kingdom

Sage Publications India Pvt. Ltd.
B-42, Panchsheel Enclave
Post Box 4109
New Delhi 110 017 India

Printed in the United States of America on acid-free paper.

Library of Congress Cataloging-in-Publication Data

Gill, Vickie.
The ten commandments of professionalism for teachers:
Wisdom from a veteran teacher / Vickie Gill.
   p. cm.
ISBN 1-4129-0418-8 (cloth) — ISBN 1-4129-0419-6 (pbk.)
   1. Effective teaching. 2. Teachers—Training of. I. Title.
LB1025.3.G454 2005
371.102—dc22   2004018167

This book is printed on acid-free paper.

04   05   06   10   9   8   7   6   5   4   3   2   1

Acquiring Editor:	Rachel Livsey
Editorial Assistant:	Phyllis Cappello
Project Editor:	Diane S. Foster
Copy Editor:	Kristin Bergstad
Typesetter:	C&M Digitals (P) Ltd.
Proofreader:	Marilyn Fahey
Cover Designer:	Michael Dubowe

Contents

Preface

I've been studying teachers since I was five years old—first as a student, then for most of my adult life as a colleague. It has been my privilege to observe many gifted master teachers who educate and inspire by their words and actions, truly making a positive difference in the lives of their students. I didn't write this book for them. This book is for those new to teaching who are attempting to define themselves as professionals, as well as for experienced teachers who have stepped into their natural role as mentors. New teachers will make many mistakes as they gain experience during their first year of teaching, but if they are perceived as being professional by their administrators, they will be welcomed back the next year; if not, their errors in judgment may be the only impressions they leave behind.

Conducting ourselves as professionals has a far greater importance than mere job security; we need to be mindful of the powerful impact that we have on our students as they develop their impressions of appropriate adult behavior. I recently read a description of a multimedia presentation titled *uBung,* written by Josse de Pauw. The audience faces a large movie screen that covers the entire back wall of the stage. On it runs a film of a group of adults at a party—laughing, joking, flirting, drinking, and later on, fighting. Standing in front of the screen on stage is a group of ten-year-olds who mimic the adults' actions in an eerily realistic manner. In Flemish, *uBung* means "practice," and de Pauw is making the point that children are observers of the adult world—watching, mimicking, and learning. This is the joy and the burden of the teacher. Many of us will be remembered as some of the most influential people in our students' lives, and attention must be paid to what we do and what we say.

In this book I offer advice about defining professionalism in teaching, locating a mentor, and figuring out what is appropriate to wear on the job. I also suggest ways to open up the lines of communication with parents, assume your role as a productive member of the staff, and avoid the petty pitfalls of gossip and resentment that occur at any place of work. Finally, I describe specific ways to use documentation to protect yourself, discuss the use and abuse of power, and suggest outlets for your continued growth as an educator. My goal is to help you create a vision of your unique self at your professional best.

I divided this book into ten "commandments" as a way to focus my writing—I do feel a passion for teaching akin to religious fervor, but this book is not associated with any religious sect or organization. Also, I use stories to illustrate my advice, but the individuals described in this book are composites of teachers I've known, and none of the names are real.

I would like to thank several people who helped me complete this book: Rachel Livsey, my editor at Corwin Press, for her encouragement and faith; Delaney Gill for her clever and intelligent critiques; and Jenny, Casey, Amy, Mark, and Kam for their unfailing confidence in my ability to be a working teacher and an author at the same time. I am blessed to have you in my life.

The contributions of the following reviewers are gratefully acknowledged:

Catherine Payne
Principal
W.R. Farrington
    High School
Honolulu, HI

Lois A. Williams, EdD
Curriculum Consultant
    (private)
Scottsville, VA

Janet Crews
St. Louis STARR Teacher
St. Louis Regional Professional
    Development Center
St. Louis, MO

Catherine Kilfoyle Duffy
English Chairperson,
    Grades 7-9
Three Village School District
Stony Brook, NY

Karen Harvey
Induction Program Coordinator
Santa Clarita Valley
    Consortium
Santa Clarita, CA

Charles F. Adamchik, Jr.
Director of Curriculum
Learning Sciences International
Blairsville, PA 15717

About the Author

 **Vickie Gill** has taught high school English, reading, and journalism for 25 years in both California and Tennessee. She has a BA in English from San Jose State University and a MEd from Vanderbilt University. She has won a number of teaching awards, community service honors, and was a finalist for Tennessee State Teacher of the Year 2000. She is currently teaching English in a small school near Santa Barbara, California. She is the author of *The Ten Commandments of Good Teaching*, which became *The Eleven Commandments of Good Teaching* in its second edition. She also conducts workshops for educators on classroom discipline, curriculum development, and the art of teaching. Contact her at vgill@juno.com to set up workshops for your school system or to discuss the ideas presented in this book.

CHAPTER ONE

Thou Shalt Define Your Terms

W hen one teacher really wants to insult another teacher, he or she will say with a slight sneer, "That wasn't very professional of you." As we head for our first teaching job, our professors wave goodbye and murmur, "And remember, above all, be professional." We nod knowingly, yet walk away without a clue as to what that specifically means. It's kind of like telling your class to "Be good!" when you have to run to the office for a few minutes. You have to define your terms. One student may think that means to read quietly in the textbook until you return. Another may think you'll be quite pleased that he didn't set anything on fire.

Based on an informal survey of the teachers, students, parents, and administrators with whom I've worked, I discovered that very few of us share precisely the same definition of professionalism. A fresh-out-of-college first-year teacher told me that professionalism is being "reserved, clear, using proper English—less slang. Following through with what you say you're going to do. Writing things down—professionals communicate in writing." My guess is that this young woman, who is only a few years older than the 12th graders she teaches, has self-consciously stumbled in conversations with older colleagues and has received one too many memos about missed deadlines. What she doesn't know is that she's caused a definite buzz around the school because she chose not to remove the small hoop that is pierced into the side of her eyebrow. A number of her colleagues dismiss her based on this one item of jewelry, and several students have grumbled about the fact that, due to the school dress code, they cannot wear piercings on their faces. Right now, she hasn't had enough experience on the job to be judged by anything other than her appearance. One definition of professionalism that would help her be successful on the job is: make sure your appearance reinforces your image as a professional at work.

A five-year veteran responded that a professional is defined by "money, accuracy, and rules," three areas that have caused her endless frustration inside and outside the classroom. She came to teaching "by accident" and does not share the attitude of most of us who are drawn to teaching: We understand that we'll never be paid what we're worth, but we thrive on a sense of earning our living by doing something worthwhile. This young woman is not teaching because she has a passion for her subject or a talent for working with young people; therefore, she searches for the correct format or rule that will allow her to wear the badge of the "professional educator." For her, professionalism will be defined by paying attention to the details and accepting the fact that she has taken on a job that is more about inspiration than compensation.

Make sure your appearance reinforces your image as a professional at work.

When I asked a 25-year veteran to define professionalism in teaching, she responded without hesitation that a professional is "conscientious, discreet, informed, and respectful." This highly honored, outstanding teacher succinctly and accurately described herself, but I would also guess that she is thinking of the legions of colleagues she has observed over the years who were unsuccessful on the job because they failed in one or more of these areas.

Next, I turned to another group of experts who have spent most of their lives studying teachers—the kids. Our students tend to be highly opinionated on the subject of professionalism and teaching. One rather rebellious high school senior offered, with a smirk, that teachers should "keep their private lives out of their job." There's a story there, but I didn't ask. Many mentioned the teacher's ability to control a classroom without being too strict and the teacher's thorough understanding of the subject matter as key issues for professionals. Very few of the students offered an opinion about how teachers dress; however, one 12th grader noted that there was "a difference between wanting to look professional and wanting to be professional. Your clothes aren't going to teach the class." I would think these students would sum up professionalism as: professionals realize that students learn far more from their actions than their words.

Of course, this survey would be incomplete without including our ultimate employers—the parents. Those with whom I spoke focused mainly on the well-being of their own children. They felt professional educators kept their children safe and engaged. They, too, looked a little puzzled when I directly asked whether a teacher's dress affected his or her ability to perform as a professional. One suggested teachers use "common sense" in choosing what to wear to school, and immediately redirected the conversation to a teacher's ability to "relate to the students and make the subject interesting—no busy work!" I believe the parents would respect this definition of professionalism: Take care of the parents and keep the lines of communication open— they have entrusted you with one of their most precious assets.

Professionals realize that students learn far more from their actions than their words.

But at the end of the day, when you accept a job with a specific school, it is the head administrator's view of professionalism that will most profoundly affect your comfort level on the job. My current principal skipped not a beat in offering his opinion of a professional educator:

> a responsible person who has the ability to work independently and manage uncomfortable situations in a healthy manner. This person meets all stated obligations, continues to grow in the profession, and displays appropriateness in all situations. Professionals model the behavior they expect to receive in return—(don't be late to class, don't hand back papers late, don't cuss). Support the policies of the institution even if they don't agree with them. The faculty meets and exceeds the dress code for all students.

Period. This man has given a great deal of thought to this issue and literally wrote the manual for the teachers with whom he will work. He fully admits he tends to see things in black and white, but in truth, what most matters to him is how a teacher's actions reflect on the school.

I always advise new teachers to approach a job interview as a two-way street. If, during the interview process, you realize that the principal's definition of professionalism is very different from your own, you'd better consider carefully before taking the job.

I can think of no more miserable on-the-job scenario than having to work under an administrator whose fundamental philosophies about professionalism differ radically from your own.

If, during the interview process, you realize that the principal's definition of professionalism is very different from your own, you'd better consider carefully before taking the job.

In order to make this decision, you must have a clear picture of yourself as a professional. In my mind, professionals show up to work on time with specific plans as to how they will accomplish the goals they have set for that day. Professional educators model the behaviors that they want their students to emulate—on the job and as members of the community in which they live. Professionals are mindful of the fact that they do not work in isolation; therefore, they treat their coworkers with the respect and thoughtfulness that they would like to receive themselves. Because they understand that the students and their parents are the customers, professional educators work to create a sense of teamwork between the school and the home.

When I accept a teaching position, I am well aware that I have been given an unusual amount of power and influence over children at one of the most impressionable stages of their lives. I need to understand the difference between true power and false power, and carefully monitor my ego so that the actions I take are based on what will help my students achieve their goals. I know that my appearance, my manners, my attitudes, and my problem-solving techniques reverberate far louder than any academic lesson I may be presenting. Before you stand in front of a classroom, you need to generate a clear vision of yourself at your professional best. I hope this book will help you do just that.

The first commandment of professionalism in teaching? Define your terms to be sure that you clearly understand and accept the expectations for a professional in your school, then work as close to that potential as often as you can.

REFLECTIVE QUESTIONS

1. Which of your own teachers came to mind as you read this chapter? What made them professional—was it their dress, their demeanor, their knowledge of the subject matter, their relationship to the students?

2. Take a quick survey of some nonteachers in your life. Ask them how they define professionalism. How does their response relate to teaching? What did you learn about professionalism in your education classes?

CHAPTER TWO

Thou Shalt Locate Your Mentor

It's easy for me to say that professionalism on the job is based on common sense, but then I have 25 years of teaching experience upon which to draw. We can all use some help, and beginning teachers would be wise to locate a mentor as soon as possible. The best mentor may not be the person assigned to you by the principal. Often the department chair or another experienced person will be in charge of meeting with new teachers to help them get started in the school year. Sometimes this works out well, sometimes not. You need to start watching from the first inservice meeting to discover the teachers who seem to have a style and perspective that you respect. This may take a few weeks, but your assigned mentor will help you with the practical issues such as attendance and ordering materials. In the meantime, talk with second-year teachers and listen in the teachers' lounge to discover the person whose style and philosophy you would most like to emulate. You'll also hear names come up over and over when your students talk about the previous year. Even though kids can be influenced by easy grades or a "buddy" teacher, over time you'll hear the same teachers' names brought up with reverence by a variety of students.

Most teachers are drawn to this profession because they like to help. Approach the potential mentor during a break or after school and ask him or her if you could discuss a few questions you have about your job. It's a good idea to let that person pick a time to meet, and it's also a good idea not to overwhelm the person with a long list of questions or general gripes. Your first meeting will be to establish a relationship upon which you can draw throughout the year. If you sit down with someone who seems annoyed or impatient with your questions, that's good information—you haven't yet found your mentor. But don't let the fear of "bothering" someone keep you from approaching him or her. I tend to be very busy when I'm at work. I rarely sit in the teachers' lounge or hang out at lunch because I have only so much energy to expend and I like to save it for my students. But I am very open to sharing materials and information with my colleagues, especially new teachers. I just appreciate having a choice about when to sit down and talk. Often I'll invite a new teacher to my house for tea and sympathy so we can discuss what's going on without interruptions. I have known several new teachers who needed the kind of help I could offer during the first few months of school, but didn't want to ask for my time. However, I can always make time and it gives me a great deal of pleasure to pass on what I know. I'm a teacher; it's what we do.

———————

Your success will be judged ultimately by what you produce and the attitude with which you approach your work.

———————

There are a number of very specific ways a mentor can ease a newcomer into the job. First, mentors can help you figure out the chain of command. This is important for survival in any profession, but essential for a teacher. A mentor can show a new teacher how to circumvent a difficult principal. Sometimes the principal is the figurehead, but the power lies with the secretaries, bookkeepers, and maintenance crew. Other than negotiating a teaching assignment or a room change, I can't think of much I need to run by my principal. I tend to view principals as my peers, often as my friends, and I try to do everything I can to make what I do reflect well on their leadership of the school. I have worked with a few principals with whom I had "creative differences." This can be annoying, but kept in the proper perspective, only a minor irritation. Your success will be judged ultimately by what you produce and the attitude with which you approach your work.

An important piece of advice a mentor should give a new teacher concerns how to create a relationship with the school's staff. These are the people who run the school. I'm happy to share what I've learned about whether a secretary can tolerate interruptions or whether a well-written note left on the desk would be more effective. I can let someone know that the head of maintenance will scowl and grumble at any request to fix anything, but that the work will be done quickly if you just smile and let him know that there's no hurry. I can clue a new teacher in to the fact that the woman who runs the cafeteria will do anything for you *if* you take the time to get to know her and her family. I can also describe the different personalities of our colleagues so that a beginning teacher doesn't make the mistake of writing off someone based on appearances or eccentricities. In other words, I can help a new employee avoid the mistakes that I've made. But I'm not likely to offer the information unless asked. So ask.

Every teacher, regardless of talent or status, has had difficult students, and it will not make you appear incompetent or ineffective to ask for help.

Another service I have performed for new teachers is to intervene with a difficult student. I teach freshmen English, so I know many of the students in the school rather well. It is a normal, regular, everyday occurrence for students to give new teachers a bit of a hard time just to check out the territory. Kids have been doing this for generations, so it's nothing to be taken personally. Most will settle down within the first week of school, but there are a few who make a career of taking advantage of tentative authority figures. I was one of those kids when I was in high school, so in many cases I can help. I would have no problem in sidling up to a student at lunch and saying, "I hear you're being a jerk in Ms. Jones' class—what's going on?" I only do this with students with whom I have a relationship and always with a smile. Then we can talk about what's wrong and how we can fix it. If I don't feel comfortable doing this, I probably know another teacher or a coach who can influence the kid. The point is that it's important to talk about problem students with your mentor early on, before a negative pattern develops that will be hard to break. Every teacher, regardless of talent or status, has had difficult students, and it will not make you appear incompetent or ineffective to ask for help. In my opinion, you should try to solve these behavior problems with your mentor before you head to an administrator for help (unless the administrator is your mentor). It's best to save the trips to the office for the most severe discipline problems.

I believe that one of my strengths as a teacher of high school students is that I remember very well what it felt like to go through adolescence. I exited high school many, many years ago, but I can easily recall how breaking up with a boyfriend makes it impossible to concentrate in class and how the desire to be accepted often clouds even the most levelheaded kid's judgment. In the same manner, after all these years, I can vividly remember how stupid I felt when I made my first major blunder as a new teacher. We have all made mistakes, so don't be embarrassed to tell a trusted colleague about a problem.

The second commandment of professionalism in teaching? Thou shalt locate your mentor. Choosing someone you respect and who respects you can turn out to be the single most important decision you will make in your first year on the job.

We have all made mistakes, so don't be embarrassed to tell a trusted colleague about a problem.

REFLECTIVE QUESTIONS

1. Was there an individual who inspired you to go into teaching? He or she was essentially your first mentor. Was it the same person you thought of in Chapter 1 as your best example of a professional teacher? If not, how did these two people differ?

2. Do you feel you have a "weak spot" in your approach to teaching? Is it in taking care of administrative tasks, like report cards and attendance? Is it in communicating your subject matter in a way that engages the students? Is it in behavioral or disciplinary measures? What kind of help or support will you need?

3. Before asking your mentor to help you with the problems you've run into, it's important to know the difference between the things you can't change (Joey's horrible temper) and the things you can change (how you will react to Joey's horrible

temper). Make a list of some problems you've run into as a teacher, then ask your discussion group to help you decide which involve circumstances your mentor can help you to change.

4. Your mentor will become frustrated if you "Yes, but . . ." every suggestion he or she offers. Make sure you know the difference between wanting to vent your frustration and wanting help with a problem. Discuss with your group the difference between a "general gripe" and a solvable problem.

CHAPTER THREE

Thou Shalt Keep Up Appearances

Some of the most powerful teachers I've known are a bit on the eccentric side and follow a highly unique vision of how the art of teaching should be performed in the classroom. They're usually easy to spot. Last year at a conference hosted by a nearby school district, I was standing around talking with several teachers during a break when one of them pointed at someone who had just entered the room and asked, "Who on earth is that?" We all turned to see a man with long, flowing white hair, dressed in jeans and sandals, deposit a large burlap bag near the speaker's podium. "Oh, my gosh," whispered a young teacher, "he looks just like Gandalf." She wasn't far from wrong. The gentleman turned out to be a guest presenter and was introduced as something of a wizard in the classroom.

At the end of the day, I spoke with a friend who had taught with "the wizard" for a number of years. She agreed that John's appearance was rather unconventional, but because of the outstanding work he's done as a middle school science teacher, he was held in reverence and awe by his students, their parents, and his colleagues. They rarely noticed how he dressed because his reputation always preceded him. A few weeks later, my friend showed me a yearbook picture of John taken in his first year as a teacher in which he looked for all the world like TV's Mr. Rogers, right down to his button-up sweater and tie. Obviously, John's appearance changed over the years, and he was able to dress in a less formal manner than most teachers. But wisely, he did not take the privilege until he earned it.

A common mistake I've noticed with first-year teachers is their inability to judge what is appropriate to wear on the job. Do you need to report to work every day in a suit and tie or will shorts and a T-shirt do? This can be very confusing to a new teacher because you will observe extremes in dress within the faculty. I've known colleagues who have enjoyed long and successful careers even though they regularly show up to work in jeans and tennis shoes. On the other hand, I worked for many years with several teachers who wore suits and ties to even the most informal gatherings. In my experience, how a teacher dresses is rarely an accurate indicator of how effective or talented that teacher will turn out to be. But not knowing how to dress professionally can cause a good beginning teacher to have a bad first year.

Before I begin to offer advice, I should point out that I can startle my students by showing up to class in a dress. One of the reasons I enjoy teaching is that 95 percent of the time I do not need to worry about what to wear to work, other than to make sure that what I have on is neat, clean, and appropriate. I, myself, rarely notice what other people are wearing unless it's outrageous or unusual. I've had colleagues pull me aside to cluck over the casualness of someone's outfit, and it's always a surprise to me. Clothing does not attract my attention, behavior does. As a mentor and as department chair, I have observed very poor teaching from someone dressed in designer clothing and have been enthralled by a lesson presented by a teacher in shorts and sandals. But the reality is that you, as a new teacher, will be judged on first impressions and attention must be paid. If you asked, this is what I would say: (1) dress for the job you would like to have, (2) err on the side of moderation, and (3) rely on your mentor for help.

In my experience, how a teacher dresses is rarely an accurate indicator of how effective or talented that teacher will turn out to be. But not knowing how to dress professionally can cause a good beginning teacher to have a bad first year.

I began teaching in the era of mini-skirts and bell-bottoms. When I accepted my first teaching job, I threw away all of my clothes and bought conservative skirts, dresses, and pants. I was 22 years old and had hair down to my waist. I looked so young that I was kicked out of the faculty lounge on the first day of school by an older teacher who didn't know I'd been hired to teach English. I was desperately trying to separate myself from the students so I could have some sense of authority in my classroom. I needed to dress in a more formal style to compensate for my inexperience. As I became more comfortable in my job and earned the reputation of a professional based on my performance in the classroom, I was able to adopt a more casual style of dress; however, casual does not mean sloppy. I work as a teacher, not a gardener, painter, or fitness instructor. If for some reason my work encompasses one of those activities, then I can dress accordingly, but this would be the exception, not the rule. When a visitor is touring the school, my appearance should leave no doubt that I am a teacher at work.

When a visitor is touring the school, my appearance should leave no doubt that I am a teacher at work.

I've talked with experienced teachers who work in schools located in economically depressed areas. They pride themselves on wearing suits and ties or dresses every day as a sign of respect to their students, who rarely see an adult dressed in such formal attire outside of church. These teachers are providing a vision of a working professional that may be lacking in their students' everyday lives. I have also worked in schools where the majority of the students come from very wealthy families and their parents often wear formal dress to work. These students are not easily impressed by appearances—for many of them, their lives are all about appearances. What they need is a teacher who will model compassion and selflessness and who will give them the gift they most need—an adult's undivided attention. So, again, it all comes down to common sense. Wearing a dress and heels will not improve my performance as a teacher. My accomplishments on the job have earned me the reputation of a professional. I am able to command a sense of authority and authenticity in the classroom without having to dress formally when I work with my students. However, I understand that parents and other visitors to the school do not know me as well, so I adjust my dress to match the situation. What I wear on a field trip and what I wear to a parent/teacher conference are not the same. I would be startled if I visited a lawyer's office and she greeted me in a T-shirt and jeans. I expect her to look the part when she is on the job.

Of course we can teach a class in shorts and sandals, but we'd be foolish not to recognize that our students expect us to look the part when we're on the job, as well. I've known young female teachers to dress so provocatively that the boys in their classes could not concentrate on the lesson at hand. An inexperienced teacher who dresses as he would in a supervisory position will have an easier time getting his students to accept him as the authority figure in the class.

Until you have enough experience to rely on your own judgment, sit down and talk with your mentor about your appearance on the job. If you've chosen a mentor whose philosophy of education is similar to your own, you can modify your dress according to his or her recommendations without compromising your self-image. The third commandment of good teaching? Thou shalt keep up appearances. Remember: If your school has a "Dress Down Day," your students should be able to notice that you're participating in the fun. If they can't tell the difference, you need to pay more attention to what you wear to school.

REFLECTIVE QUESTIONS

1. What is your vision of yourself at your professional best? What are you wearing? Is it the same thing you wear in the classroom now? Why or why not?

2. As a student, how much attention did you pay to what your teachers wore? How did that affect your experience in their classrooms and your respect for them as educators?

3. Discuss the dress code that you had to follow when you were in high school—which rules did you support and which did you wish you could change? What is the dress code for teachers at your current school?

CHAPTER FOUR

Thou Shalt Respect Your Power

Mandatory inservice sessions and our regular weekly teachers meetings are a challenge for me. I'm just not good at sitting for long periods of time and passively listening, especially if the topic does not capture my attention or it's about something I already know. My mind often wanders, my feet wiggle, my body fidgets, and if the meeting is particularly long, I'll slowly slump down until my six-foot frame ends up in a wedge-shape hovering precariously on the edge of my seat. And if the same person brings up the same unsolvable complaint that she brings up every week, usually just as the meeting is about to be adjourned, it's everything I can do not to stand up and scream at her to either fix it or zip it. But I don't. I'm a professional. Part of my job description mandates regular attendance at these meetings; I knew that when I accepted the position. So I pull it together, take down the information I need, and head out to do the best job I can. After all, that's exactly what I expect my students to do, even when they're in a class they find boring. It would be hypocritical of me to model behavior for which I would admonish them. In a way, the weekly faculty meetings remind me to be patient with restless students, to keep my lessons relevant, and to eschew busy work.

I often tell new teachers that students learn far more from watching what we do than from listening to what we say. I believe that having to be a consistent role model is the single most difficult part of teaching and parenting. It's exhausting, but kids are experts at spotting hypocrites, and when they do, they are merciless in exposing them. I have been in disciplinary hearings where a student who has been caught drinking at school takes great delight in describing his father's drinking habits to all of the adults in the room. I have watched in horror as an enraged teacher backed the school bully into a corner, using threats to persuade the student to control his temper. The student backed down, but the lesson he took from the encounter was not what the teacher intended, rather it reinforced the misconception the student had about the true nature of power in the first place.

I often tell new teachers that
students learn far more from watching
what we do than from listening to what we say.

Teaching is a difficult job—it can be frustrating and relentless in the demands that it places on our lives. We all need the ego boost that comes with the sense that the students like us. Truthfully, that is probably the single most difficult hurdle a beginning teacher faces.

Returning teachers are known entities. Either the students have been in their classes before or the kids have heard about the teacher from a friend or an older sibling. Experienced teachers have a backlog of lessons from their "Greatest Hits" file that they know will be well-received by the students at that specific grade level in that specific school. However, new teachers have to start from scratch, and I always warn them that the first few months will be tough as the students try to figure out what they can and can't get away with. Many of us have had the experience of introducing ourselves to a roomful of teenagers only to receive yawns or glares in return. It takes time and much effort to establish a meaningful relationship with our students, and the temptation to get them on our side as soon as possible is hard to resist.

Over the years I've observed many new teachers try to make friends with students by acting like a buddy. This often backfires because—News Flash—we're the adults, they're the kids. A couple of years ago I watched this scenario unfold itself like a three-act play. Jerry accepted the job as a visual arts instructor for the high school. He was approaching 30 years of age, but he dressed like a 17-year-old, in baggy pants and "Bob Marley Lives" T-shirts. He carefully mastered the art of indifference and dishevelment in his appearance, and the students were enthralled from Day One. He made fun of school rules, telling the kids that school should not feel like a prison, and ignored petty issues like coming to class on time. He let the kids define the curriculum based on their interests and they decorated the room with their favorite posters, words, and images—some pressing hard against the border of inappropriateness.

It takes time and much effort to establish a meaningful relationship with our students, and the temptation to get them on our side as soon as possible is hard to resist.

Many of the older teachers bristled at the mere sight of Jerry and spent a great deal of time talking about him behind his back. I tried to remain open-minded when I listened to the kids rave about his class, but I worried about where he was headed because I'd seen this scenario played out before. The principal kept an eye on things, but was impressed by the students' enthusiasm and by several conversations he'd had with parents who praised Jerry for turning their kids on to learning in such a dynamic way. The first quarter ended with an impressive display of creative projects produced by his students, most of whom received an "A" for the first grading period.

By the end of the second quarter, Jerry was having a real problem with kids missing 10 or 20 minutes of his class. He'd received a number of complaints from parents who questioned the validity of the curriculum or who were shocked by the subject matter of some of the films the kids had produced. As things became difficult, Jerry pulled the kids around him even more tightly because he badly needed their support and undying loyalty. He invited the kids to his house on the weekends to watch movies. He forged close friendships with some of the biggest discipline problems in the school, often driving them downtown to eat sushi or prowl through used record stores. The adults were becoming more and more uncomfortable with Jerry as a colleague, but in his students' eyes, he was a god.

Predictably, when the third quarter rolled around, Jerry was forced to become accountable for his actions inside and outside the classroom. Until the bitter end, he viewed many of the teachers and the administrators as dinosaurs who were obsessed with rules and regulations with no real understanding of the needs of the kids. Jerry left the school with a flourish, giving a speech in which he encouraged the students to "stick it to the man." The students dedicated the yearbook to him and there were many tears as his car pulled away from the school for the last time. But he missed the denouement.

At the beginning of the next school year, a number of his most faithful followers took great delight in telling all who would listen that during movie night at Jerry's house, he often drank beer while the kids were munching on popcorn. Several girls regaled their friends with stories of how Jerry would smoke in his car and shout obscenities at the idiot drivers in front of him. By the end of the year, Jerry was often referred to as a joke and someone started a rumor that he'd had an affair with a student. This is sad, because in talking with Jerry, he really did like the kids and wanted to open their minds and teach them some truths about life. But the lesson the kids ultimately learned is that he himself could not make his own life work.

I believe Jerry had the potential to be a good teacher—he was intelligent, brought great energy and excitement to his classroom, and viewed the students as people rather than names listed on a roll sheet. His was an error in judgment—he didn't realize that the students have all sorts of friends who can show them how to be a teenager, but what they needed from him was an example of how to be a "cool" adult who performs his job in a professional manner. He hadn't met the kids in a mall or at a family barbeque—he'd gotten to know the kids in his role as their teacher, and even when he hung out with them outside of regular school hours, the kids thought of him as a teacher who had become a friend, rather than a friend who had become a teacher. It's a big difference.

This does not mean that a teacher cannot be silly, funny, and friendly in front of the students. I have known teachers who go to the other extreme and adopt such a severe demeanor that the classroom turns into a battle zone. Although I have watched scores of "buddy" teachers like Jerry come and go over the years, I see far more new teachers flounder as they desperately try to set themselves up as the authority figure over students who can see that it's all an act. Every year I assign a piece of literature that naturally generates a discussion on the nature of power. I introduce the concept of false power versus true power early on so that I can refer to these terms throughout the year. To begin, I ask the students to describe a "powerful" person, and I write the words on the board as they call them out. Inevitably they'll mention great physical strength, crafty intelligence, the biggest gun, a sexy appearance, and unlimited wealth. Then I'll distribute a quote from Sigmund Freud that says, "We display outrageously and obsessively that which we do not fully possess or have deeply at our disposal." We talk about the bully who has great strength, but is powerless when he is outnumbered or injured. His power rests solely on his ability to physically overwhelm all challengers. I suggest that true power rarely calls attention to itself, and once established, does not have to be constantly proven.

I suggest that true power rarely calls attention to itself, and once established, does not have to be constantly proven.

When I ask teachers to define power in the classroom, they often visualize a room full of obedient learners who yell, "How high?" in unison when the teacher shouts, "Jump!" I know a few coaches who can pull this off without a hitch, but in my experience, this type of false power will backfire. There is no doubt that on the first day of school, the teacher needs to take control of the classroom. Most of this is done months in advance by careful planning to figure out exactly what you want the students to do, when you want them to do it, and what will happen if they don't. Anticipation is everything in classroom management. A class starts out with teacher control, but very soon it needs to morph into self-control on the students' part. The way I know I have achieved true power in a class is that the kids do exactly what I expect them to do whether I'm there or not. This is accomplished by making sure the students clearly understand and accept the value and usefulness of what I am teaching.

It's easy to intimidate students—we have failing grades, demerits, detention, and expulsion on our side. But the kids have plenty of ammunition in their arsenal as well: indifference, sabotage, stealth, lying, cheating, and silent harassment. In the end, the teachers will win the war, but the students will win the battles. I have counseled many bitter teachers who proudly display a long string of F's awarded to the behavior problems in their classes, but it's cold comfort at the end of a miserable year. One of the worst things a teacher can do is to set him- or herself up as a one-dimensional teacher rather than a real person who has something significant to teach.

I would think that everyone who becomes a teacher is drawn to the profession because of the kids. When we reminisce about the highlights from our years of teaching, very few of us will generate a sentimental tear over the piles of tests and essays we corrected. The stories we tell over and over will be about our students—their highs and lows, their struggles and successes. Many of us will keep in touch with former students long after they graduate from school, and we will be mentioned as having been one of the most influential people in their lives. This is a huge honor and a huge responsibility.

One of the worst things a teacher can do is to set him- or herself up as a one-dimensional teacher rather than a real person who has something significant to teach.

It's important to forge friendships with your students—we're in a people business and each of the students has a story to tell, but the only way you'll be allowed to "read" that story is to deal with the students in an open and friendly manner. However, you do not have to interact with the student as a peer to be his or her friend. After the students exit the school, they will forget many of the facts they've memorized in your class, but they will remember the example you set of how a personable, successful person conducts himself on the job. And they'll like you for that. The fourth commandment of good teaching? Thou shalt respect your power; for many of the kids, you may be one of the few people in their lives who model how a grown-up should behave.

REFLECTIVE QUESTIONS

1. Would you lean more toward viewing your classroom as a battlefield or a playground? If you answered battleground, what steps can you take to adjust your approach and "lighten up" a little? If you answered playground, how can you establish more of a leadership role with your students?

2. What classroom situations make you feel powerless? How will you deal with this? What is your reaction to powerlessness in other areas of your life? Will these reactions transfer to the classroom? Why or why not?

3. Share examples of false power and true power with your discussion group. How does the quote from Sigmund Freud relate to teaching?

CHAPTER FIVE

Thou Shalt Take Care of the Parents

I try to relate every lesson I teach my students to real life situations. One of my favorites is on the ability to recognize the balance of power in any given situation. I ask my students to draw a flow chart indicating the power chain in our school system. Inevitably the students will place the School Board at the top and the students at the bottom, but I turn this upside down to help them understand that everyone employed in a school district works for the students and their parents. The kids are usually gleefully surprised. This perception of power often makes other teachers feel uncomfortable, particularly those whose authority rests on false power. But for me, it's the perfect response for when the kids grumble that I work them too hard: "That's why you hired me, to improve your reading and writing skills." They shake their heads and roll their eyes, but somehow this helps them refocus on why they are in school in the first place.

So, I consider my students' parents to be my bosses, and I do what I can to keep them happy. Truthfully, it isn't all that hard. Parents are hungry for information about their children, but some find teachers to be intimidating or overly busy. My favorite method of communication is an e-mail. I find it to be quick, cheap, easy, and because it's in the form of a note, it's not as laborious to write as a letter. One of the first homework assignments I give is for each student to have his or her parent or guardian e-mail me before the end of the first two weeks. The beginning of a school year is a good time to do this because the parents are still highly interested in what's going on at school and, hopefully, it's too early for major conflicts to have occurred. If some of the students' parents do not have e-mail accounts, I ask those kids to ask their parents to write a short note or to telephone to let me know how I can best communicate with them. For an e-mail response, I compose a generic "I'm glad your child is in my class" paragraph, then add a sentence to personalize the note for each kid and hit Send. My students' parents are thrilled—sometimes shocked—that I'd take the time to do this, and a positive tone has been set for the year. Often the parents will give me inside information about a difficult time a student is going through that helps me understand confusing behavior in the classroom. I can gently broach a discussion about inappropriate actions before the situation gets out of hand.

I'll let you in on a secret I've
learned over the years: Most parents
love their kids, want the best for their kids,
and want to be perceived as good parents.

Some of my students are horrified that I've opened a line of communication with their parents, but I let them know that we work as a team to ensure their success. I'll let you in on a secret I've learned over the years: Most parents love their kids, want the best for their kids, and want to be perceived as good parents.

We can all come up with an alarmingly long list of horrendous parents who have done far more damage than good in their children's lives, but parents who are there to receive an e-mail from a teacher want to do the right thing even if they don't know how to do it. The trick to dealing with difficult parents is to search for the meaning behind their words. I find guilty parents to be the most difficult; these people usually have a contentious relationship with their kids at home, and some try to make up for that by storming into the school to "set that teacher straight" about little Johnny. Parents are often looking for a magic fix for their out-of-control children. They desperately search for the right school, teacher, or curriculum that will "fix" their kid. This always makes me feel uncomfortable because even though I have tried to develop a number of effective methods for improving a child's communication skills, I have no magic wand. After all of these years, I firmly believe that the greatest predictor of a child's success in school is the quality of the instruction going on at home. That said, it is still my job to accept every child sent my way, and to work to make sure each has progressed in the skills I teach when exiting my class at the end of the year.

———•◆•———

Parents are important to my success as a teacher, so I am going to do what I can to take care of them.

———•◆•———

Parents are important to my success as a teacher, so I am going to do what I can to take care of them. Back to the concept of picking and choosing our battles: I cannot change a parent's personality, but I can help modify how a parent perceives his or her child's progress in my classroom. In my current school I work with a number of students for whom English is their second language. I am often in awe of these students' abilities to speak, read, and write in another tongue since I am not bilingual. Whenever they get frustrated, I ask them if they'd like me to show them what I can do in their language—this usually gets a laugh. English is an exasperating language to learn because many of the rules of grammar and syntax appear illogical and random. Try explaining to an Asian student when to put "a, an, or the" in front of a noun in English (I live in "the" United States, or I live in "America"). This can be very confusing and frustrating, but over time, as the students become familiar with the cadences and idioms of their second language, the problems smooth themselves out. But many of their parents were raised in a culture where anything less than excellent is unacceptable. I cannot tell you the number of conversations I've had with parents who demand that their children earn no less than an "A" in high school English, regardless of the child's proficiency in English. I try to get them to marvel at their child's accomplishments and point out that an A would represent an excellent command of the English language, a B an above average command of the language, and a C is average.

I find a writing portfolio to be an essential tool that will clearly trace improvement on the child's part, but also illustrate how much work remains before excellence is achieved. I've known teachers who award A's to highly motivated ESL students based on how hard they work, rather than their mastery of the subject. This will keep the parents happy, especially when the child is trying to build an impressive GPA for college applications, but this can backfire on you, the child, and the parents.

Recently I ran into a student who had graduated from my high school three years earlier. He was never in my freshmen English class, but I knew him as a member of the student body. When he was in high school, Gerald maintained a 4.0 GPA and scored well on his SAT's. He was accepted by a top college, and his parents were pleased. However, he told me that his college graduation had been delayed a year because he had to take a remedial English class in his freshman year. In high school, Gerald had struggled with in-class essays, but turned in flawless papers that were obviously edited by someone else. His teachers gave him A's in English based on his work ethic, pleasant manner, and earnestness, but I could tell that he felt cheated when he was forced to take a class for no college credit because it was a prerequisite for many other classes he needed to take in his major. Gerald's parents felt well taken care of as they watched their son pick up top honors at his high school graduation, but I wonder how they felt a year later.

Just as it is not productive to hand out high grades to keep parents happy, it's a mistake to use grades to punish bad behavior. It can feel very satisfying to write a great big F on a report card to get back at a kid who has been torturing you for months, but that will rarely fix the problem. In the first place, students who are disruptive in class are probably disruptive at home, too. It's unlikely that the parents have enough control over their children to effectively modify their behavior in your class based on the fear of a failing grade. More likely, they'll transfer the blame by attacking you and your teaching methods. I've seen this happen over and over. You need to intervene in a problem like this at the earliest opportunity, before the situation gets out of hand. Luckily the parents of obnoxious children cannot read our thoughts, otherwise they would have seen, "Little Billy is one of the biggest brats I've had the misfortune to know in many a year!" flashing through my mind. As tempting as it would be to call a spade a spade, that will not create the sense of teamwork you'll need to help Billy succeed in your class.

———•◦•———

Just as the most difficult students we deal with are kids who feel like failures in the classroom, the most difficult parents we deal with are those who feel like failures at home.

———•◦•———

Usually you can spot potential behavior problems within the first two days of school. It is essential that you contact the parents immediately to say something nice about Billy so they know you are the one teacher who recognizes the untapped potential of their little boy. It's a great idea to do some pretesting early on so you can talk about specific skills that need to be improved, as well as point out strengths that you've noticed. Truthfully, students who act up in class are often covering for learning difficulties, inappropriate problem-solving skills, or poor self-esteem—often it takes some real creativity to come up with a strength, but you can do it. "Billy is always the first one in class." "Billy has so much energy!" or "Billy brought his binder to class two days in a row." Later on, when you have to speak to the parents about poor classroom behavior, they'll remember that you did start out on their son's side.

Just as the most difficult students we deal with are kids who feel like failures in the classroom, the most difficult parents we deal with are those who feel like failures at home. You cannot change their home situation, but you can change how the parents view their child's progress in school. This goes for high achieving students as well as those who struggle academically. You are not demanding perfection in either case, but you are asking the children to work as close to their potential as possible, as often as possible. By carefully monitoring your students' progress and regularly reporting this progress to the parents, you can make the parents feel essential to the team. This is why I like e-mail as my main form of communication with parents. It's quick and far less intrusive than a phone call. Some of your parents will not have e-mail accounts or even home computers, in which case you'll have to rely on a note sent to the house. If I have a situation like this, I'll call the parents and tell them that I'll be sending a note home every Wednesday so they'll be sure to look for it. As a last resort, I'll use phone calls when I have no reliable way to communicate in writing with the parents. But regardless of how difficult it seems, I have to keep in mind that I work for the parents and it is my job to keep them updated on what I'm doing with their children.

We all love good stories and we are civilians outside of school hours, but talking about other teachers, students, administrators, or parents can cause a great deal of harm.

If you live in the community where you work, you will likely run into your students' parents outside of school. Chatting in line at the grocery store can be a great way to build goodwill between the parents and you, but you have to be very careful to avoid gossip. Again, we all love good stories and we are civilians outside of school hours, but talking about other teachers, students, administrators, or parents can cause a great deal of harm.

I will often have parents come up to me to complain about another one of their child's teachers. As in every work place, there are a few bad apples and it would be easy for me to comfort the parent by agreeing that, yes, Julie's math teacher is a jerk. In fact, I probably have all sorts of stories I could tell about what I consider to be inappropriate behavior on the part of the math teacher, but even if I'm friends with the parent outside of school, I am offering my opinion, which is often based on hearsay or insufficient information. Eventually, it will get back to the math teacher that Julie's mom and I were talking, and even though it will make Julie's mom understand that her daughter is not the only student having problems in math, it will not fix the problem. Go back to the simple "treat other people like you'd like to be treated" concept—I would very much resent a colleague talking about me behind my back without giving me a chance to present my point of view.

Even after school hours, when you are in the community, you are a representative of your school. You may be angry with your principal over some slight, but running him or her down in public serves only to reflect badly on the school, your place of employment. As a professional, you need to monitor how you air your differences with your coworkers because ultimately it will reflect poorly on you. Whenever I talk with someone who insists on telling me a secret that they were holding for someone else, I walk away from the conversation realizing that this is a person I cannot trust with my secrets.

---

*Even after school hours,
when you are in the community,
you are a representative of your school.*

It's the same for gossiping with parents about your colleagues or other students—I would imagine that they would walk away wondering what you say about their children when they're not around. Hopefully, you have close friends or family members who are willing to be sounding boards for you. Tell them all of the wild, angry stories if that will keep you from talking to more casual acquaintances about those with whom you work. But be careful about telling these stories to your own children if they attend the same schools. The stories will come out and you may be called in to justify some comments you made in passing about one of your students, a student's family, or your colleagues.

When you are at work, remember that you're accountable to your administrators, but that your true employers are your students' parents. You can create a great deal of goodwill by communicating with them often and appropriately, and they will back you when problems arise. Remember that grades are nothing more than an indicator of a student's mastery of certain skills during a specific block of time. Be careful not to use grades to appease the parents or punish their children. The time you devote to establishing regular, positive communication with the parents will pay off later in the year. The fifth commandment of good teaching? Thou shalt take care of the parents—healthy teacher/parent relationships will prove to be the greatest job security you can have.

REFLECTIVE QUESTIONS

1. How can you create a sense of teamwork with the majority of your students' parents? What are specific things you have done or can do to open the lines of communication between home and school?

2. How do you deal with gossip at work?

3. Sit down with a partner and draft the opening lines of an e-mail you could send to parents after the first week of school.

CHAPTER SIX

Thou Shalt Pull Your Weight

S tudies by Harvard, Stanford, and the Carnegie Foundation suggest that success on the job depends 85 percent on people skills and only 15 percent on technical knowledge. That's a remarkable statistic; since teachers are in a people business, I would think that percentage would be even higher for educators. When I was designing a Vocational English program for a Tennessee school district, I interviewed a number of presidents and owners of major companies in middle Tennessee. I asked them to tell me what they wanted me to teach my students in my high school English class. Not one of them mentioned grammar or Shakespeare, but they all very plainly stated, "Teach them how to work cooperatively with other people."

When you are hired to work in a school, you immediately become a member of a team—even if you are the only person who teaches a particular subject. I often think that a hallway in a typical school is very much like a neighborhood. It is true that you can live for many years in a house and never speak to the people who live next door to you, but in my mind that lack of communication makes your life so much more difficult.

People who work in a school share the same facilities, supplies, students, and bosses. You may be the most self-reliant person in the world, but there will be a time when your responsibilities cross over into another person's responsibilities, and it will be so much easier if the two of you get along.

I often think that a hallway in a typical school is very much like a neighborhood. It is true that you can live for many years in a house and never speak to the people who live next door to you, but in my mind that lack of communication makes your life so much more difficult.

A few years ago I worked with Julia, an administrative assistant who was very good at her job. She was efficient and thorough and rarely made mistakes. Julia communicated with most of the staff through memos or e-mail and had an office to herself. She didn't seem to need or want friendships on the job, and she could be rude when someone interrupted her to ask a question or forgot to respond to a note. Her coworkers wouldn't dream of asking Julia to help with a task that wasn't specifically outlined in her job description—she'd either refuse or complain the entire time she was working. However, Julia also had small children, and as with any working parent, emergencies arose. I witnessed Julia asking someone to cover for her while she took her child to an appointment of some sort, and her requests were either dodged or grudgingly fulfilled. Julia had good intentions, but because of her cold, dismissive demeanor, very few people were receptive to her input. Even worse, the students would have nothing to do with her, which is akin to a salesperson who cannot get customers to return her calls.

Teachers are hired to teach specific classes and specific subjects, but they will be asked or required to participate in all sorts of extracurricular activities as part of the job. Just as in choosing how friendly to be with students, I've seen teachers who go from one extreme to the other when asked to help out. First there are the "it's not in my contract" types. If they're asked to help monitor students at an assembly, supervise kids on the playground, or attend a brainstorming session on a new program for the school, these teachers let everyone know how unhappy they are or complain so much that someone else picks up the extra duty. This may save you time, but it will cost you in goodwill later on when you need help. A good question to ask yourself when you're required to do something extra is, "If I don't do it, who should?" There are many tasks that make a school operate smoothly that no one wants to do.

A good question to ask yourself when you're required to do something extra is, "If I don't do it, who should?" There are many tasks that make a school operate smoothly that no one wants to do.

In my school, students who earn too many demerits are required to do an afternoon work crew. The school staff takes turns monitoring the group to make sure the jobs get done. Sometimes when I'm showing a 16-year-old how to empty a garbage can without making a bigger mess than was there already, I think, "Nine years of higher education to prepare me for this?" But when it's my turn, I step in and do my part, because it's the right thing to do. I don't keep track of the hours of extra duty I put in compared to the hours put in by the math teacher down the hall. I have faith that there's a system in place and that it will all work out. I also know that I can spend more time complaining than it would take to just do the job.

In direct contrast to the complainers are the martyrs. These people sigh and take on the tasks that have been assigned to people who do not show up, making sure everyone else feels their misery as they do the extra duties. Even though they work twice as long as anyone else, they can be just as annoying as the complainers. I will actually stop a martyr from picking up a job left by a slacker by telling her, "If you do this now, Joe will expect you to do it every time. Why should he ever do something he doesn't want to do if he knows you'll step in and cover for him?" A common comment is that Joe won't do it right if he's forced to pitch in, but I try to point out that

Joe's incompetence is an administrative issue that will not come to the attention of the administrator until we stop enabling him.

I work for an administrator, Susie, who outworks everyone else on campus from the janitors to the headmaster. Whenever I feel like grumbling about monitoring another study hall, I think about the fact that Susie approaches every job with a positive attitude, does it to the best of her ability, and rarely complains or assesses blame. Sometimes she ends up doing a job that should have been done by someone else, but many of us work extra hours for her because she sets such a good example herself. She is free with her time and encouragement, and many of us are anxious to return that favor to her. She has many, many deposits in her goodwill bank, and when she needs help, she has credit to spare.

It's easy to get bitter about the inadequate salaries or the interference of state agencies in our curriculum, but if you accept the job, you need to show the students the best version of your productive self that you can.

Which brings me to another pitfall for teachers. We teach in isolation and are the masters of our domains. The quality of what happens in the classroom depends on our motivation and inspiration. Teaching is an unusual job in that we can get away with very little work in the privacy of our classrooms, especially if we're easy on the grades. It's simple to slip in a video that vaguely relates to the subject matter or assign "silent reading" in the textbook while we correct papers. The students will cheerfully go along with a slacker teacher because they're kids, but the truth will come out. Kids talk to other kids, other teachers, and parents—we will be held accountable for our teaching methods and the progress of our students. This is absolutely as it should be—we're trained professionals working to the best of our ability for as much of the time we have as possible. It's easy to get bitter about the inadequate salaries or the interference of state agencies in our curriculum, but if you accept the job, you need to show the students the best version of your productive self that you can. This includes handing back student work in a timely manner—it's hard to nag a student about late homework when you return their tests and essays weeks after the assignment was given.

When I was in college preparing to become a teacher, the classes I loved best were about literature or writing. I can remember an hour flying by as we dissected a poem or marveled at the syntax of a Henry James novel. I visualized myself standing in front of a group of eager teenagers holding a copy of *The Great Gatsby* in my hand and saying, "Let me show you why I love this book." But first I had to take attendance and post it outside the door; then I had to record tardies and decide which excuses were good enough for a reprieve. Next, I had to read to the class a revision in the student handbook outlining the rules for parking in the student parking lot, and make sure every student understood the new expectations by having each person sign a contract, which then had to be sent to the front office. Gatsby had to wait.

---

*A key element to professionalism
on the job is meeting deadlines.*

I am no fan of paperwork; I find much of it annoying and repetitive. But I know that if I fail to turn in certain forms or submit my grades late, I am causing some secretary a lot of extra grief. A key element to professionalism on the job is meeting deadlines.

I've seen report cards delayed for several days because one teacher failed to get hers in on time. I've witnessed the frustration of secretaries who are trying to compile a report because one teacher failed to turn in his section. If you think about it, very few people who work in your school ever enter your classroom. The only impression they have of your competence is hearsay from the students and your reputation for having things completed on time. Teaching is an unusual job in that our lives are run by bells. We time our tasks to start and begin within seconds of a bell, and unless a meeting is held after school, we all have someplace we need to be at any given minute of the day. If you are late to meetings, if you miss appointments, or if you are constantly behind with your paperwork, you will generate a great deal of resentment among the rest of the staff. Make it a point to be early and get things finished ahead of time, so when the inevitable interruption, emergency, or technical snafu arises—trust me, the copy machine always breaks down before final exams—you'll still get the job done on time.

It is essential to protect your individuality as a teacher, but you have to accept the fact that you do not work in isolation. Whenever you're asked to pitch in as part of a team, close your eyes and picture how you would like someone to respond to you if you had asked for help. Or even better, remember how you felt the last time you asked a student to straighten the chairs in your room and the student responded as if you'd asked him to scrub out all of the bathrooms in the school. Don't do that to your coworkers. The sixth commandment of good teaching? Thou shalt pull your weight. As I tell my students over and over, it's not all about you.

Make it a point to be early and get things finished ahead of time, so when the inevitable interruption, emergency, or technical snafu arises—trust me, the copy machine always breaks down before final exams—you'll still get the job done on time.

REFLECTIVE QUESTIONS

1. Do you agree with the statement that 85 percent of our success on the job is related to our people skills and only 15 percent depends on our job-related skills? Why or why not?

2. Are you a complainer or a martyr? Or are you more like Susie?

3. How will you keep up with your paperwork yet hold yourself accountable for using your time in the classroom to the best advantage for your students? Do you have any timesaving or organizational tips for other teachers?

CHAPTER SEVEN

Thou Shalt Pay
Attention to the Details

When I was a child and I failed to do a chore properly, my father used to say, "The devil is in the details," then make me redo it a little more carefully. This was one of the most useful lessons I learned in preparing to become a teacher. Successful teachers understand the importance of anticipation, preparation, and documentation. Sometimes it seems like the United States has become "The Land of the Litigious," and teachers can be vulnerable to lawsuits. It's important to make a habit of maintaining accurate, up-to-date records and keeping them in a secure place.

Teachers do not enjoy the luxury of sorting through applications and deciding which students they would prefer to work with each year. One of the glories of our public school system is that we educate everyone; one of the frustrations of working in our schools is that we educate everyone.

Children with diagnosed behavior disorders are mainstreamed so that they can associate with students who display appropriate behaviors. I'm a big fan of this law, but I also know that one difficult student can dominate and disrupt an otherwise good class. You cannot just kick these kids out of your room. In my opinion, it's a mistake to take them to the office repeatedly or to have an administrator come into your classroom to intervene except in the most severe cases. Part of a good classroom management program is to establish yourself as the authority figure, which means you'll have to try to handle almost all of your discipline problems by yourself. This is one of the ways you'll begin to build your reputation as a professional in your school.

The first step is to anticipate problems and have a well thought-out set of rules and consequences in place before the first day of school. The next step is to spend a great deal of time in the first two weeks making sure your students clearly understand the rules and the consequences. The third step is to create a discipline file for your documentation. The fourth step is to be consistent in your discipline so that an infraction is quickly and calmly followed by the appropriate consequence.

Part of a good classroom management program is to establish yourself as the authority figure, which means you'll have to try to handle almost all of your discipline problems by yourself. This is one of the ways you'll begin to build your reputation as a professional in your school.

A basic rule in my class is, "Don't disturb other students." I'm aware that experts advise us to phrase all rules in the positive, but this is exactly what I want to say. As a young teacher, I fell into the trap of saying, "No talking" or "Don't get out of your seat," but I soon learned these were impossible to enforce fairly (are you really going to punish a student for quietly asking a neighbor for an extra sheet of paper or for getting up to pick up a pen that dropped on the floor?). But I can demonstrate to my students what it means to disturb a class. During the first week of school I explain the rules, then I act them out in an amusing way; by the end of the first week, the students clearly understand what I need them to do. The students sign a contract that lists the rules and consequences and states that they have "read and understand" my expectations (they don't have to agree with them, just indicate that they understand them). After we've reviewed them several times, I give the students a short-answer quiz on the rules and consequences with the expectation that everyone will get an A as their first grade of the school year. If a student answers some of the questions incorrectly, I have him see me outside of class until he can write the correct responses. I then file these contracts and quizzes in my Classroom Management file.

If a student disturbs the class (this means the student's actions were disruptive enough that they drew my attention from the task at hand), I give him (or her) a verbal warning, always said in a calm, matter-of-fact voice: "Joey, I need you to turn around and rejoin our group." If Joey creates a disturbance again, I'll very quietly hand him a "reflective essay," which gives him the chance to mull over his actions, the problems they created, and what he'll do in the future to correct the situation. The next day Joey hands me the signed essay, and I never bring it up again. But this goes in the Classroom Management file as well.

I taught with a very talented teacher in Tennessee who used a slight modification of this system in his Exploring Technology class. Steve would hand the student a small form that asked for the student's name, the date, and a single sentence describing the infraction—this was signed by the student as well. He'd thank the kid and place it in a special file. This is a powerful form of documentation. Problem children often tell their parents that a teacher is "picking on me," and the parents will ask for a conference with the teacher to find out what's wrong. Steve used to enjoy these conferences. He'd sit there politely while the student claimed that every time she got in trouble it was someone else's fault, sometimes adding that Steve just "doesn't like me." Steve would wait until the student and the parents had their say, then draw forth the disciplinary folder, dramatically dumping its contents onto the table. Out flew all sorts of little slips of paper with sentences detailing each infraction in the student's own handwriting, with a signature and the date to boot. The problem was usually very quickly resolved after that.

In my classroom, if a student ever argues that he didn't understand that he needed to have his materials with him every day or there'd be a consequence, I can look puzzled and pull out the student's rules quiz, saying I thought for sure I'd given him full points for that answer. I try to keep it light, but the students know I mean business and that I will be fair and professional when I deal with discipline problems. I also carefully document every phone conversation and print copies of e-mails that I send or receive from parents, so that, if necessary, I can clearly demonstrate what I've done to try to resolve the problem with the student and with the parents. In my experience, most administrators will back you up when you are accused of dealing with a student ineffectively, but you would be very wise to have some documentation to support your position.

A professional teacher has a plan, does not take things personally, and carefully documents any situation that could be called into question later. I have seen teachers in serious hot water over not reporting what appeared to be a slight injury on the playground. Recently I dealt with a teenager who slipped and bumped her head on the sidewalk. I wasn't there, but her friend brought her over to me and I could see that she wasn't badly hurt. However, I contacted the school nurse, filled out an accident report, and notified an administrator. Kids are prone to all sorts of bumps and bruises, and it is impossible to predict which ones will be minor and which ones will need serious medical attention, so I carefully document each incident. It may seem like a waste of my time, but I know how much time it will cost me if complications arise and I have not covered my bases carefully.

A professional teacher has a plan, does not take things personally, and carefully documents any situation that could be called into question later.

One of my favorite units to teach involves technical writing. When I introduce it, I wear a button that says, "Assume nothing"— this is great advice for taking care of the details of our jobs. I advise new teachers to keep a calendar and carefully record every meeting or extra duty as soon as they receive a notice about it. Do not assume that someone will remind you of an obligation. Do not assume that some paperwork due at the end of the month can be turned in on the last day. In many secretaries' minds, the end of the month starts on the first day of the last week of that month—double check. Do not assume that you can take your students to the library without reserving that time with the librarian. Do not assume that you can leave some money you've collected from your students in a sealed envelope covered up by a pile of papers in the bottom drawer of a filing cabinet that sits in a closet at the back of your classroom. The kids will find it. Do not assume you can leave a little early if you don't have an end-of-the-day class. I don't think you should become paranoid and stress over the tiniest "what if's," but it's wise to double check on due dates, meeting times and locations, and modifications of the rules.

Another assumption you have to be very careful about making concerns plagiarism. I would imagine since the earliest days of formal education, students have presented someone else's work as their own. Sometimes this is done unintentionally, sometimes it's a blatant act of theft, but you have to move with caution when you suspect a student of cheating. On the simplest level, spread the kids out as much as possible when they work on an in-class test. Try to design your assessments so they consist of more than multiple-choice questions, requiring the students to display what they know in writing.

Papers written outside of class can present more of a problem. The Internet has become a powerful tool for students working on a research project, but it's a huge temptation to just download a paper or copy and paste large blocks of text. Teachers who require very little in-class writing from their students might have a difficult time determining if the paper they are grading was indeed written by the student. Some of my colleagues have had great success using a search engine like Google.com to expose plagiarism. All you need to do is type in a line or phrase from the suspect writing, and if the resource is on the Internet, there's a good chance Google.com can find it.

Keeping a portfolio of samples of individual student writing is another effective tool. Last year I watched a bright young teacher raked over the coals by irate parents because she accused their child of plagiarism without preparing her case. She was an English teacher and very familiar with the student's writing, but she had not kept any samples of previous writing from that student. After the parents demanded a meeting with the principal and the young teacher, she came to me for help, but since I was her department chair (and mentor), she should have come to me first. She showed me the writing in question and I had no doubt that she was right, but a Google.com search turned up nothing. The writing was suspicious because the syntax and diction abruptly changed mid-paper, but the young woman had no solid proof except a gut feeling that the student had copied the passage from a book or some other resource.

I did what I could to defend the young teacher and to placate the parents, but without specific evidence, she didn't have much of a case—except for the fact that I think everyone in the room knew the child had copied the work, including the parents. But their daughter had told them that she felt inspired by the topic and it brought forth the best writing she'd ever done. When asked to show the group samples of her previous writing for that subject, the girl dismissed the request by saying she threw everything away because she "hated that class."

After things calmed down, I talked with the young teacher to help her figure out what to do the next time something like that occurred, but I could tell that she'd be gun-shy about questioning plagiarism by her students in the future. The steps she should have taken start long before the paper was assigned.

First, the teacher should have built a writing portfolio of in-class writing samples that could be used to trace progress over the semester. This would be a valuable resource if a student's writing seemed radically different on a particular assignment.

Second, she should have designed the topic of the essay to make it difficult for students to easily locate a pre-written paper on the Internet. Instead of asking the students to write about the death of the American dream as illustrated in *The Great Gatsby,* which could come straight out of *Cliff Notes,* she could have asked the students to compare Gatsby with a character from an unrelated novel, like *This Boy's Life.* The purpose of the essay, I assume, would be to assess the student's understanding of the concept of the American dream, to allow the student to prove that she or he had read the assigned novels, and finally, to determine whether or not the student understands how to format and write a formal essay.

Third, check out a search engine to see if you can find the source before any accusations are made.

Fourth, when faced with a question of plagiarism, any teacher would be wise to ask the advice of a trusted colleague—get someone else's opinion. It is very possible that you are so burned out from reading so many badly written essays, that you become wrongfully suspicious of an outstanding effort on a student's part. If your mentor agrees that the writing is suspicious based on the evidence you've amassed, then you have a choice. If the evidence is overwhelming, you can present the information to an administrator so that she or he can initiate disciplinary actions or you can meet with the student one-on-one, and give the student the opportunity to rewrite the paper for a reduced grade.

Whichever course you choose, you have to keep in mind the desired outcome. I've participated in a closed meeting with a teacher, a student, and me in the role of department chair in which the teacher's suspicions about plagiarism were raised, and the student chose to rewrite the paper. This young lady was a top student who recently had been accepted by a prestigious college and had cracked under the pressures of a course load that included four AP classes. She admitted her mistake, listened to a discussion about what would happen if she repeated this lapse in judgment in college, and thanked the instructor for giving her a chance to redo the work for a much lower grade.

This young woman could have been expelled from school for her mistake, which means she would have lost her place in the university. I'm not sure that's the lesson she needed to learn. It was more important for her to realize that the easy way out took much, much more of her time, and that passing off a few paragraphs as her own writing almost cost her everything she'd worked so hard to achieve.

If you want to be respected by your colleagues, show up to meetings on time and complete your paperwork before it's due, if possible. Again, very few of your coworkers will actually watch you teach, so the impression you make on them will be in how well you handle the little things. Even though careful documentation will take up some of your precious spare minutes, amassing clear evidence that you did the right thing at the right time in the right format will save you hours and hours later on—and could mean the difference between retaining or losing your job. The seventh commandment of good teaching? Thou shalt pay attention to the little things. As my (much more positive) mother would say, "God is in the details."

REFLECTIVE QUESTIONS

1. How can you tell the difference between a classroom situation that you can handle on your own and one where you should consult an administrator?

2. Work with someone who teaches at the same grade level you will teach to create a list of no more than five classroom rules and five related consequences that would form the foundation

for your classroom management plan. Be sure to be specific, especially with the consequences.

3. Have you ever dealt with a question of plagiarism? How did (or how will) you handle the situation?

CHAPTER EIGHT

Thou Shalt Pick and Choose Your Battles

W e teachers are experts in conflict resolution. Kids can be verbally and physically abusive to one another, and it is our job to diffuse these confrontations before they get out of hand. But one of the worst verbal assaults I've witnessed over the years was between two teachers. A student told Colleen (history) that Sylvia (health and PE) had said something negative about Colleen in front of a group of students. Colleen marched off to confront Sylvia, who was in the office checking her mail. The two women shouted at each other for a while, then Sylvia walked away. Colleen followed her into the next room where I was leaning against the Xerox machine happily making copies of an upcoming vocabulary test. I was startled (but secretly amused) by the names these adults were calling each other. The argument escalated into a litany of accusations that went back several years. I tried to make a lame joke to distract the women, but it took the intervention of an administrator to calm them down. This would have been funny if it hadn't been so pathetic. Petty disagreements will always occur on the job. How we handle them is a clear indicator of our level of professionalism.

We all love to tell stories, and teaching is a business that generates fascinating, very human tales. In fact, a powerful teaching technique used by many master teachers is to illustrate a point by recounting a true-life occurrence. However, we adults need to pick and choose our audience carefully. We are not machines, and after a particularly frustrating day, it is necessary to vent to someone so our anger doesn't remain bottled up inside. Sometimes our families are a little burned out with listening to our woes, or our friends get tired of trying to feign interest in our complaints about people they don't know in a job they've never experienced. Our best audience is our coworkers; we all know one another, we're all interested in what happens in our workplace, and we have enough inside information to truly enjoy some really good gossip. But care must be taken. Stories have a way of sliding along the grapevine at lightning speed, and they will come back around to you.

Petty disagreements will always occur on the job. How we handle them is a clear indicator of our level of professionalism.

I have been in the very sticky situation where my complaints about a particular student were overheard by a coworker who, unbeknownst to me, was a second cousin to the parent of the child. I was simply griping, but I suddenly found myself having to defend ill-phrased remarks to people who were not amused that I was talking about their offspring in such a casual manner. All I could do was apologize, but the damage was done.

We do not work in isolation and we work with a wide variety of personalities, so disagreements are inevitable. We need to think very carefully about how we will handle these conflicts before we're in the middle of one. My best advice to teachers, students, parents, administrators—anyone who works with people—is to learn to pick and choose your battles. I often illustrate this to my students by spreading a big pile of papers, pens, pencils, and books all over a table. I tell them that these objects represent some of the petty annoyances all of us face every day. We could choose to react to every one of them, or we could save our anger for the ones that really matter. I'll randomly pick up a pencil and say, "This is when someone bumped into me in the hall." I put it down, then pick up a paper, "This is when I received an F on a quiz for which I did not study." I put it down and pick up a pen, "This is when I heard that a girl in my science class had said something nasty about my boyfriend." I put it down. I hold up another piece of paper, "This is when I saw some seniors picking on a much smaller freshman," and I dramatically fold the paper and put it in my pocket: "This is a battle I choose."

—•—

It surprises my students to hear me say that one's temper is an honor to behold, but I make the point that the minute I lose control over my emotions—and that's what happens when we lose our tempers—I have given control of myself to another person.

—•—

Next I hold up one hand, spreading the fingers wide, and tell the students that these fingers represent my chosen few—people I love and trust enough to give them the honor and privilege of seeing me lose my temper. I have exposed myself to these individuals so that they know me intimately—they are the recipients of my greatest strengths and weaknesses. They have the power to make me excessively happy or irrationally angry, but I do not hand that privilege to just anyone. I ask my students to think about how often they lose their tempers in a given day, and point out that some of them are giving that great gift to everyone indiscriminately.

It surprises my students to hear me say that one's temper is an honor to behold, but I make the point that the minute I lose control over my emotions—and that's what happens when we lose our tempers—I have given control of myself to another person. I tell the kids that the easiest type of student to discipline is one who does not have mastery over his or her emotions. In the same way, the easiest type of teacher to torture is one who is easily angered.

Over the years I've worked with a number of teachers who pride themselves on their volatile personalities. These "tell it like it is" types blow up on a regular basis and let anyone within hearing range know that they will not be taken advantage of. If you try to talk to these people and point out the kinds of problems they create for themselves, they just shrug and say, "That's just how I am." Then I ask them if they would accept that answer from a student who screamed at them in a classroom. I've known a number of talented teachers who become on-the-job jokes to their colleagues because of the fact that they get mad at everything. No one takes them seriously, even when their anger is justified. When we overreact to a perceived slight or a sense of being taken advantage of, in truth it is probably our insecurities rather than our sense of fairness that is being triggered.

The first thing to do when you have a problem with a coworker is to identify what you can and can't change. Trust me, often you can't change your coworker's attitudes or actions, but you can change how your coworker's actions affect you. Let's look at some specific examples: (1) You notice that the teacher in the room next door comes to work late every day because he doesn't have a first period class. You resent this because you are never late, even though you have far more demands on your time in the mornings. Is this a battle you should choose? No, it's an administrative problem. (2) Another coworker is rarely in class when the late bell rings, and her students mill around in the hall, which creates a distraction for your students. Choose this battle—it's worth fighting.

When we overreact to a perceived
slight or a sense of being taken advantage
of, in truth it is probably our insecurities rather
than our sense of fairness that is being triggered.

You might protest and say that it is not fair that the teacher in the first scenario gets away with being late when our contracts specifically stipulate that we are supposed to be at work one-half hour before classes begin. But if you go through the day trying to monitor the fairness factors for the entire school, you'll only succeed in making yourself bitter and generating a great deal of resentment from your peers.

You should try to alter the second scenario. The teacher's tardiness is interfering with your effectiveness as a teacher, but how will you approach her? Ideally, you'll keep it at the discussion level where you state the problem and let her know how it affects you. This is where "I" messages are very effective: "I'm having a hard time getting my students to focus on the lesson I'm presenting because they're watching these other students fool around in the hallway. I'm getting frustrated and I need your help." The first step is letting the other teacher know that there is a problem in the first place. We all have different levels of tolerance for chaos.

When I sit down to a desk cluttered with books and stacks of papers, I cannot think until I straighten the mess, but I have friends who produce outstanding work from under piles of old magazines and half-eaten sandwiches. It is very possible that your coworker would not bat an eye if another teacher's students were peeking in her window—she'd just wave and go on with the lesson. So, it's imperative that you let her know that it is a problem for you in as nonaccusatory a tone as you can possibly muster. In truth, you're not trying to make your colleague feel incompetent; you just want the best shot at engaging your students in what you've planned to teach that day.

Another way to avoid losing your temper on the job is to train yourself not to take things personally.

Frank Zappa, lead musician for The Mothers of Invention, once said, "I'm happy to outrage anyone who chooses to be outraged." I keep that quote close by because it's easy for me to lose perspective at times, and I want to have a sense that I save my anger for the most worthy battles. I am not going to blow up because someone took the pen out of my mailbox for the tenth time, but I will intervene with eyes ablaze if I witness someone in a position of power bullying someone in a weaker position. I rarely lose my temper, so when I do, people tend to pay attention.

Tammy, a language teacher, storms into the principal's office at least once a day bellowing about some infraction of a rule or a perceived insult. She is rarely taken seriously, and the principal told me that he sometimes pretends to be on the phone when he sees her coming. Once again, your anger is too great a gift to give to just anyone. Save it for the battles that are worth fighting.

Another way to avoid losing your temper on the job is to train yourself not to take things personally. If you went out of your way to do something to annoy a colleague and your coworker attacked you verbally, I would think it would be far more productive to try to figure out why you provoked this person rather than to get in a fight with him or her.

I often tell my students that the best indicator of how people feel about themselves is evident in how they treat other people. Unpleasant people often harbor truly unpleasant feelings about themselves. A person with a good self-image gets no pleasure out of causing other people to feel badly about themselves. If a student walked up to me and said, "I hate you!", I'd never respond with, "Well, I hate you, too." Unless I've done something on purpose to make that student hate me, I'd probably think, "Whoa, Angie's having a bad day," and I'd try to find out what happened. I've spoken with colleagues who have taken great offense because another teacher walked past them without speaking. This is one of those situations where your reaction tells far more about your own low self-esteem than about the thoughtlessness of another.

I often tell my students that the
best indicator of how people feel about
themselves is evident in how they treat other people.

On any job, we all will deal with difficult people. Sometimes, after getting to know someone, I recognize that I will be able to interact in a productive manner with that person on many different levels—professionally and personally. With others I have to carefully define the parameters of our encounters. It is very possible to find a way to work with people whom you find unpleasant or unreasonable. You just have to control your responses to them and waste very little time trying to control them. The eighth commandment of good teaching? Thou shalt pick and choose your battles. Save your energy for the far more worthy task you've accepted, which is to educate your students.

REFLECTIVE QUESTIONS

1. Think about the last time you lost your temper with someone on the job. Was it over a personal insult or general irritation? What was the outcome of the confrontation?

2. How can you best remind yourself to hold your temper and maintain control in a tense situation? Some books suggest creating a mantra that you can repeat to yourself when you are getting close to losing your temper. (I use the image of a yappy dog to amuse myself until the other person calms down—this helps me to keep it from feeling like a personal attack.)

3. In your situation, which battles are worth choosing?

CHAPTER NINE

Thou Shalt Grow in Your Profession

I hate to say it, but teaching is one of the few professions where a person can get away with practicing his or her craft in the exact same way for 30 years. I read somewhere that Rip Van Winkle could wake up 100 years later, enter a school, and recognize exactly where he was—very few other businesses are like that. English and math teachers can prepare their students for the SAT tests with only slight modifications in the curriculum they've taught since they entered the profession. I used to work with a longtime history teacher whose course outline covered ancient civilizations to the Renaissance, and he often used the same handouts and lecture notes that he'd developed when he was a student teacher.

As an English teacher, I know my goal is to improve my students' reading and writing skills, and quite honestly, I can do that with the same novels I read when I was in high school. Most experienced teachers have a magical "bag of tricks" from which they've drawn for many, many years—lessons, classroom demonstrations, and field trips that perfectly illustrate the point of the lesson at hand. I would never suggest throwing out an activity just because it's been done before; however, I would recommend that teachers constantly search and study within their discipline to locate new "magic."

It's hard to believe, but I still work with teachers who resist embracing the computer as a vital tool for an educator. Twenty years ago I realized that incorporating word processing into my English classroom would allow me to work in small groups with my students. I also found computers to be a great asset for kids with learning disabilities. All of these years later, I'm still the only English teacher in my school with ten computers in my room. My colleagues are gifted literature teachers and I would never force technology on them, but word processing programs have allowed me to assign far more writing than before because (1) I can read it quickly and (2) I can ask the students to revise and revise again until they master certain basic writing skills. In my opinion, this is where the real learning takes place and the process isn't as laborious as rewriting an entire essay. I'm also aware that most of the writing my students will do on the job later in their lives will be done on a computer. What we teach in our classes must keep up with the changes in what our students will be required to do when they exit the school system.

Just as in any profession, teachers must subscribe to journals and attend conferences related to their discipline. It's important to keep up with the latest research, and hopefully you will grow in your profession to the point that you have something new to present at a conference or submit to a journal. At least once a year I'm required to attend an inservice meeting about learning differences. It is astounding to me that anyone in our profession would not be aware of the mounds of research produced over the past ten years about the fact that we all access information in different ways. Yet every year I watch my colleagues zone out when a demonstration on learning styles is presented.

What we teach in our classes must keep up with the changes in what our students will be required to do when they exit the school system.

True, I get restless because I'm a believer and they're preaching to the choir in my corner, but during the break old George, who has taught social science for 25 years, will grumble, "Ah, the kids are just lazy. If they'd shut up and listen harder, they'd pass the class." Even when he participates in activities that clearly show the difficulties a visual or kinesthetic learner experiences in a straight lecture format, he dismisses the information as "coddling" the kids.

I have seen a dramatic increase in the number of students I teach who have diagnosed learning disabilities, and I'd be remiss if I didn't work to keep myself abreast of the latest research available to improve the way I present information to these kids. This would be akin to a doctor who insists on invasive surgery to perform a biopsy rather than becoming informed about laser techniques.

Partly due to the system of tenure, every school carries mediocre or sometimes incompetent employees, which is why I advocate radically raising teachers' salaries to make our profession highly competitive. We can get away with performing at a level far below our potential for many, many years—it's up to us to monitor our own growth.

It's important to stay abreast of what is happening nationally and internationally in our profession, and to relate the information we are teaching to the big picture. As we become master teachers, we need to make a point of passing our knowledge on to others in the roles of mentors, writers, and presenters. Teachers enjoy a certain type of job security in that there will always be children to educate, and because this is a difficult job and the pay is not commensurate with the amount of training required, there will always be a need for educators in almost every community in every region of the country. However, a far more satisfying employment insurance comes from building a solid reputation as an effective and innovative educator.

We can get away with performing at a level far below our potential for many, many years—it's up to us to monitor our own growth.

Another tool for growing in your profession is classroom observation and evaluation. All of us dread being criticized, and it's normal to stress over being "on" when an administrator visits our room to evaluate our teaching. We can dismiss the whole process by wondering how valid a 50-minute observation could be in judging our performance for the entire year, but any feedback is good. Unless something horrendous happens, it's unlikely your job will be in jeopardy. It's always good to find out whether or not you're doing what you think you are doing.

Whenever I go into another teacher's classroom to observe, I try to make the whole experience as relaxed as possible, but I'm looking for certain things. Before the observation I'll ask the teacher to tell me specifically what she or he would like the students to accomplish by the end of the period. I also ask the teacher to describe what will occur in class that day.

I've been told one of the most useful things I do is quickly make a list of all of the students in the class, then tally every time a student speaks, indicating whether it was voluntary or involuntary. Often I'll have teachers say that the class will discuss a certain topic, when in reality, only three very vocal students and the teacher speak. Ideas fly around the room, giving the appearance of a classroom discussion, but the tally sheet helps the teacher see that only a small portion of the class was actually engaged in the lesson. Another suggestion I make is for the teacher to ask the students to write one sentence describing the most important thing they learned during class that day. This can be painfully revealing or highly gratifying, depending on the quality and accuracy of their answers.

——————————

It's a waste of time to take offense at an evaluation. It is very possible that the evaluator got it wrong, but just as when a friend becomes angry with something I did, I wouldn't react to the anger as much as wonder what it was I did that made my friend think I had offended her.

——————————

I always make it very clear that I can report only on what I saw on one particular day, at one particular time, during one particular class. I know the teachers want to earn an A—just as their students want to do on any given assessment—but my observation can be far more useful than a ranking of excellent or good. In looking over the report I hand him, a new teacher can feel confident that certain techniques produced the expected results. If I did not observe an outcome that the teacher thought was clearly evident, the teacher can contemplate why that wasn't clear to me. It's a waste of time to take offense at an evaluation. It is very possible that the evaluator got it wrong, but just as when a friend becomes angry with something I did, I wouldn't react to the anger as much as wonder what it was I did that made my friend think I had offended her.

A good evaluator can be a powerful sounding board as you grow in your profession. In the same manner, it can be very helpful to ask a friend to sit in on your class to observe in an informal manner. A fellow English teacher can offer me all sorts of tips that will improve my performance, but a science teacher could be a great resource for me to find out if the lesson I'm teaching is producing the results I predicted. The science teacher will observe my class with few preconceived notions about the subject I'm teaching and can offer feedback about how well I'm communicating. I once helped a new teacher from another department solve major discipline problems simply by suggesting she rearrange the desks in her room. Finally, students can provide you with the most specific, accurate evaluations of all.

At the end of each quarter, I take time to ask the students to reflect on what we studied and the usefulness of the information. At the end of each school year, I collect a written evaluation about the most valuable and least valuable units I presented over the past ten months. I tell them that I will not read the evaluations until my final grades are submitted, so what they say will not help or harm their GPA in any way. I have used these student evaluations to fine-tune my English curriculum over the years, and in my mind, they are the most valid critiques I receive.

Students can provide you with the
most specific, accurate evaluations of all.

I sincerely hope that anyone entering the teaching profession is embracing a career rather than accepting a job. Despite the frustrations of less than professional-level salaries and the fact that a promotion in teaching often means leaving the classroom, you will spend most of your working days improving the lives of children. If you choose to accept this awesome responsibility, I hope that you will actively work to improve your skills and increase your knowledge in this dynamic field. The ninth commandment of good teaching? Thou shalt grow in your profession. Keep abreast of what is happening in other schools and conduct your own research based on the data you collect in your own classes. One of the best examples we can set for our students is that of a lifelong learner.

REFLECTIVE QUESTIONS

1. What is the most valuable feedback you've received from a classroom observation? Have you ever been in the situation

where you and your evaluator had different perceptions as to the effectiveness of a particular lesson you taught?

2. What efforts do you make to stay abreast of the news and advances in education? How have you incorporated this material into your curriculum?

3. Describe the most stimulating and informative professional conference you've attended. What did you learn that you now (or will) use in your classroom?

CHAPTER TEN

Thou Shalt Be Yourself

I t's been my privilege to be the official and unofficial mentor to a number of new teachers. I talk with them early in the school year to make sure they can articulate their expectations for classroom behavior, as well as specifically describe what it is they want the kids to know when they exit their class at the end of the year. Often I'll share copies of my rules and consequences; I even go so far as to act out why I feel some rules are impossible to enforce and what I do when a student breaks a rule in my class. The main point I want to get across is that I have an elaborate plan that is simple to execute. I encourage new teachers to develop their own classroom management program before the students arrive. In the past, I've had a few teachers just photocopy my rules and hand them out to the students on the first day. The results are often disastrous. It took me several years to devise my system for classroom management, and it was truly a process of trial and error. I finally found a method that matched my personality and that made complete sense to me, and I've been fine-tuning it for 25 years. The biggest problem I see when beginning teachers adopt someone else's discipline plan is that they are not willing to follow through with the consequences in a consistent manner. These teachers need to gather as much advice as possible, sift through it, and come up with a set of rules that feels comfortable to them and that they will enforce without hesitation.

There is nothing more painful to watch than a teacher in front of an out-of-control class tossing out empty threats: "If you do that again, I'm going to send you to the office!" "Do you want to go to the office?!" "I'm serious, stop that or you are going to the office!" The class is watching to see who will blink first, the unruly student or the teacher. They know that this is a clear indicator of who is in control.

Develop an individual teaching style
that showcases your strengths rather than
your weaknesses. Don't try to be someone else.

I use humor and affection, laced with a forceful personality, to maintain discipline in my classroom. It is not likely that I will back a student against the wall or throw him out of class to assert my power; however, my students know I mean what I say. But a young teacher with a passion for her subject who has a quieter demeanor should not try to copy me—it won't work. She needs to use far more subtle techniques like guilt (hey, it works) or creating a desire to protect her in the most aggressive students in her class. I have seen this in action and it's very effective. Visualize the best version of yourself as a teacher based on your unique talents and personality, and ask your mentor to help you devise a classroom management program that will allow the students to see that side of you. The teacher down the hall may flourish as the tough, "don't smile until Christmas" martinet because the students value what he teaches. Another colleague may accomplish all of her objectives by being the "fun" teacher who runs a loose, but productive program. Develop an individual teaching style that showcases your strengths rather than your weaknesses. Don't try to be someone else.

Especially when you are fresh out of college, it's not unusual to feel as if you are playing a role—it wasn't too long ago that you were the student watching the teacher, and now you've changed places. As you attempt to become comfortable in this new skin, beware of donning the mask of the "faux-professional." I've seen teachers correct other teacher's grammatical constructions when they're talking across the lunch table. I knew a young man who crossed out every contraction when proofreading his colleagues' reports to the parents, forgetting that these were notes that would be mailed to a home, not dissertations to be submitted to a committee. I've watched with amusement as new teachers set themselves up as the pillars of professionalism by criticizing their peers' style of dress, speech, record-keeping, coaching—you name it. I always want to whisper in their ears, "Your insecurities are showing," because I know that we tend to overreact to that with which we struggle most in ourselves.

The person you need to monitor is yourself, making sure that you are living up to your vision of a professional—leave the nagging to the administrators. The best sermon you can deliver is through your example. If the way you conduct yourself on the job is effective, you will influence others. Otherwise, what you say will more than likely just produce resentment.

Also, the most successful teachers I know are careful to build a life for themselves outside of school. You will not last long as a professional in this business unless you take care to have a private life.

We could teach 24 hours a day and still not do everything we are capable of doing. Our jobs are never finished because our students continually change and grow from the day we meet them until the day they leave our classes. There will always be the kid who needs extra counseling, extra tutoring, extra coaching. I never fail to enter the last month of a school year in a sense of panic over how much more I need to teach the kids before they're ready to move on. A real concern in the field of education is teacher burnout. I became interested in mentoring new teachers because of the distress I felt when I watched a high percentage of them quit after the first year.

---◆◆◆---

You will not last long as a
professional in this business unless
you take care to have a private life.

---◆◆◆---

Many of your best friends will be fellow teachers, but I encourage you to find friends who know nothing about education and prefer not to listen to you discuss it for hours on end. Every once in awhile I'll go out to dinner with a group of teachers from my school, but we have a rule: Anyone who brings up a topic related to our jobs has to put a dollar in the middle of the table. The waiter takes home the money along with the tip. Most of us enter teaching because we love kids—they fascinate us. We become experts in the subject we teach, spending a great deal of time adding to our expertise. It's easy to become "one-trick ponies." Another role we are modeling for our students is that of the well-rounded individual—we need to go out and seek experiences outside of our profession.

Another role we are modeling for our students is that of the well-rounded individual—we need to go out and seek experiences outside of our profession.

As a young teacher, I would often assign major essays or research papers to be due a day or two before vacation so I could have the extra time to grade the students' work. I quickly learned that that was a big mistake. Teachers have regular vacations built into the school year because teaching is a performance art and we have no understudies. Teachers are on the go from the minute they enter the school until they turn out the bedside light after correcting the last paper. Use your vacation time to read for pleasure, to pursue a hobby, or to do nothing. If you can, travel to some place where you are not likely to be recognized. I love my students, but it makes my heart sink if I hear, "Hey, there's Ms. Gill!" when I'm on vacation. I need the break. There are times I invite students over to my house for an informal gathering, but I make sure they understand that my family and I need privacy. I don't have an open-door policy at home and I screen my phone calls. I'm available for emergencies, but my definition of an emergency and my students' definitions often do not coincide. When you report to your job, I hope you have developed a strong work ethic where you give the best you have as often as you can. But when you are not at work, allow yourself to relax. You'll be far more productive and last longer in the profession.

When you accept the challenge of becoming an educator, you step off into one segment of your hero's journey. You will be tested, you will triumph, and you will fail. But along the way you will pick up the tools that will help you become a true professional. The teacher's path is the perfect analogy for Joseph Campbell's philosophy because you seek enlightenment, and then you return and share it with the community.

The average person will spend 90,000 hours working in his or her lifetime. You have chosen a profession in which you can earn your living, but more important, you've chosen work that matters. You will teach your students how to become professionals later on in their lives by the example you set on the job.

When you report to your job, I hope you have developed a strong work ethic where you give the best you have as often as you can. But when you are not at work, allow yourself to relax. You'll be far more productive and last longer in the profession.

I can't imagine anyone wanting to become a teacher unless she felt she had something authentic and valuable to pass on to her students. Keep that in mind as you interact with your students and your colleagues. The tenth commandment of good teaching? Thou shalt be yourself—just make sure it's the best version of yourself as a professional educator.

REFLECTIVE QUESTIONS

1. Why did you become a teacher in the first place? What unique qualities will you bring to a faculty?

2. How will you separate your home life from your school life? How will you manage to grade all of those papers without taking time away from your family and friends?

Afterword

*T*he *Ten Commandments of Professionalism for Teachers* should be a prerequisite for all teachers before they are permitted to enter a classroom, to help them develop a sense of judgment about how a professional behaves on the job. In fact, teachers with years of experience would also benefit by reading this book, as it would help them to evaluate their skills and performance better in the classroom. In today's business environment, teaching is also a critical skill required by corporate employees in their dealings with clients and peers, as well as for government officials who deal with the public. They, along with anyone in a leadership position in any organization, would benefit from this book. The advice that Vickie Gill offers is direct and to the point, and it is basic enough for anyone to understand and benefit from. *The Ten Commandments of Professionalism for Teachers* presents a commonsense, "blue-collar" approach to dealing with the personal behavior that is required for teaching success.

This book provides a discussion of the professional behavior that is needed for strong leadership, so its value extends far beyond the relatively confined limits of the classroom. Leadership is a personal quality that is important to every organization that faces change, and change is a fundamental need for everyone who is trying to deal with the global economy. It is no longer sufficient just to be a doer, it is now necessary to think before you do, and then to be able to explain the process that you are following clearly enough so that others can follow. Vickie Gill's book outlines the type of leadership and teaching skills that are required to manage the ongoing process of change.

Teachers have long needed to master the leadership qualities necessary to give students the confidence to face change and to "gamble" on the effort required to "think" in new ways. Whenever anyone is involved in change, the possibility of failure (and opportunity) exists. Society usually penalizes failure, so the common reaction of most people is to retreat to old ideas and old solutions, even if they are wrong. A teacher in this new educational environment is required to help students to think and to learn in ways that permit the questioning of ideas and actions. This process of critical analysis exposes students to an increased risk of failure, so the management skills that are needed for this teaching process become increasingly more challenging. In fact, the very future success of our society is dependent on the new forms of instruction that are developing as a result of the significantly expanded availability of information and the increased computer skills of the new generation. In this context, Vickie Gill's book fills a real need to help teachers guide their own development.

A number of years ago, I was asked to give a "State of American Education" briefing to a former President at the White House, and in the middle of one of the presentations, the President fell asleep. So I spoke in a loud voice and said, "We have found a way to eliminate baseball in the United States, Mr. President." With that the President quickly awoke out of his sleep and grumbled, "What was that you said, Professor?" I went on to say that he would eliminate baseball by "teaching it in the public school system." Now interested, the President leaned forward and said, "Explain." So I suggested that they would teach the rules of the game in first and second grades, teach the physics and mathematics of ball trajectory in third through sixth grades, then in middle school they would teach the economics of baseball and the history of the sport—maybe even visit a ball field and hold a baseball and bat. In high school they would concentrate on the advanced mathematics and physics principles of the sport. Then at graduation the students would (if they passed the final exam) be allowed to go on to a baseball field and play the game. He replied, "In ten years, you would eliminate baseball in the United States!"

We can see the drawbacks of a single-variable type education in the way that our companies and our government are run. The problem is that the information age has brought with it a need to manage better the solution to multivariable and complex technical, social, and political issues that require resolution not as a fixed pronouncement, but rather with constantly changing answers as the issues start to get resolved. In other words, teaching the process for seeking a solution to a problem became just as important as the solution itself.

Several years ago, I enjoyed watching the reactions to an experimental History program that was developed to illustrate both sides of the American Revolution in a teaching program; it included an equal portion of readings from both English newspapers and American newspapers of the time. The traditional teaching approach in American schools was to present this history always from the American point of view. The student controversy that developed when the English side was presented clearly illustrated the point that the standard textbook on the subject was not a fair purveyor of the knowledge, and that the merits of the other side needed to be considered.

By understanding both sides of the problem there was significant student discussion, and strong opinions developed in this classroom. The teacher managed the discussions to encourage the students to think about the issues of the Revolutionary period of our history rather than writing down selected dates and facts. The classroom teacher had to change her persona totally to deal with these students properly. A teacher in this situation would have benefited from reading Vickie Gill's book. The *Ten Commandments of Professionalism for Teachers* provides teachers with the guidelines of personal behavior that are needed to function properly in this new and evolving educational atmosphere.

The information age has also dramatized the fact that when students receive a college degree at a commencement ceremony, this might be the end of formal classes, but it is really the beginning of a lifelong learning process. To survive, American businesses have initiated ongoing educational programs for the growth of their employees, because education must be continuing if the employees and the company are to stay current. In effect, everyone with any management responsibility has now become a teacher in our new society. Because of this change, Vickie Gill's book is important to anyone involved in education, and not just to classroom teachers.

The evolution of education has moved teaching from a profession where the teaching job involved dispensing facts, to the present situation that requires a teacher to manage and moderate discussions that encourage students to think. Thinking is hard; students are required to take chances where they might fail, and failure is something that everyone tries to avoid. Therefore, this new form of teaching requires real leadership on the part of the teacher if the student is to manage failure, grow from the experience, and then change things to achieve success. It is the "master teachers" of our society who help to move our culture to higher levels. It is books like this that provide the insights necessary to help ordinary teachers develop into "master teachers."

Neal Mitchell, *former Professor*
Harvard Graduate School of Design

CORWIN
PRESS

The Corwin Press logo—a raven striding across an open book—represents the union of courage and learning. Corwin Press is committed to improving education for all learners by publishing books and other professional development resources for those serving the field of K–12 education. By providing practical, hands-on materials, Corwin Press continues to carry out the promise of its motto: **"Helping Educators Do Their Work Better."**